# **Time Management**

Attain Proficiency In The Art Of Time Management,
Overcome And Prevail Over Procrastination, And
Enhance Your Productivity

*(The Essential Principles Of Time Management For
Individuals With Hectic Schedules)*

**Klaus Kloiber**

# TABLE OF CONTENT

Maximizing Time Efficiency ................................... 1

Determining What Your Long-Term Goals Are . 8

Taking A Look At How You Currently Manage Your Time ........................................................... 28

Planning Your Time Wisely For The Day .......... 50

Establishing Favorable Patterns Of Behavior . 72

Dull Work And Activities With A Low Priority ........................................................................... 84

The Importance Of Self-Control And Perseverance In The Process Of Habit Formation .............................................................. 98

Effective Means Of Working Together And Communicating ........................................... 105

Delegation Of Duties .............................................. 118

Conquering Your Tendency To Put Things Off ........................................................................... 154

## Maximizing Time Efficiency

Having gained a comprehensive understanding of the concept of time, let us now delve into pragmatic approaches for effectively maximizing its utility.

Outlined below are several strategies that can assist you in maximizing the efficiency of your time utilization.

Establishing precise objectives: It is imperative to establish clear goals in order to effectively focus our efforts and optimize our use of time.

By establishing precise and quantifiable objectives, you are imbuing your daily endeavors with a distinct sense of direction.

Pose this question to yourself: What is the desired outcome I intend to accomplish? What are the necessary procedures to attain the desired outcome? The possession of a distinct vision pertaining to your desired achievements will facilitate task prioritization and deter futile engagements, thereby conserving time.

Identification of activities that yield significant value: It should be noted that not all tasks possess equivalent influence on our lives.

Certain items hold a higher degree of significance compared to others.

Effective time management necessitates the identification of activities that yield substantial value.

Evaluate your obligations and duties, and prioritize them according to their significance and impact on your objectives.

Direct your efforts and allocate your time towards endeavors that yield significant outcomes and are in consonance with your objectives.

Minimization of disruptions: Distractions pose a formidable obstacle to optimal productivity and efficiency.

Thoroughly analyze the primary sources of disruption within your professional or everyday surroundings, and implement measures to effectively mitigate their impact.

Disable cellular phone notifications, designate a scheduled time to attend to electronic mail and social media, and establish a workspace devoid of disruptions.

By reducing external disruptions, you will enhance your ability to concentrate on tasks, leading to increased productivity within a shorter duration.

The Pomodoro technique: This methodology proves to be a highly efficient approach to optimizing work productivity by effectively managing time.

This methodology encompasses the subdivision of time into concise intervals of labor, typically lasting 25 minutes, subsequently succeeded by brief periods of respite.

Maintain unwavering concentration on a singular task without any disturbances during every designated work interval.

After the completion of every cycle, it is advised to indulge in a brief respite in order to recuperate and renew one's vitality.

This method facilitates the preservation of focus, mitigates cognitive fatigue, and enhances overall productivity over the course of the day.

Organizational practices: The art of organization is integral to the achievement of efficient time management.

Acquire the knowledge and skills necessary to effectively utilize organizational tools and techniques, including but not limited to the utilization of to-do lists, agendas, or calendars, in order to strategize and manage your activities and priorities.

By possessing a well-defined sense of purpose and direction, one can effectively circumvent the dissipation of valuable resources and efforts on tasks lacking relevance or necessity.

Arrange your tasks in order of their significance and immediacy, concentrating on endeavors that yield the greatest outcomes.

Efficient management of individual time: While prioritizing productivity and accomplishing tasks is vital, it is equally imperative to allocate time for self-care, leisure activities, and relaxation.

Maintaining an equilibrium between professional responsibilities and personal commitments is crucial for optimizing time allocation.

Allocate time towards endeavors that foster both your physical and mental wellness, such as engaging in physical activities, practicing meditation, pursuing hobbies, or spending meaningful moments with cherished individuals in your life.

Please bear in mind that allocating time for oneself should not be viewed as a luxury, but rather as an imperative for rejuvenation, maintaining motivation, and achieving equilibrium.

By implementing these strategies in your daily routine, you will acquire enhanced proficiency in managing your time in a productive and proficient manner.

Please bear in mind that effective time management is a continuous endeavor that necessitates honing one's skills, adapting to changing circumstances, and exercising self-control.

Through the recognition of the importance of time, the establishment of precise objectives, and the application of pragmatic approaches, individuals will embark on a path towards attaining significant outcomes and deriving utmost satisfaction from each passing second.

## Determining What Your Long-Term Goals Are

Establishing enduring objectives is a fundamental aspect of establishing significant goals and efficiently managing one's time. Long-term objectives encompass the intended results one seeks to attain within an extended timeframe, typically spanning from one to five years. Outlined below are several methods for establishing your long-term goals:

1. Articulate your vision: Ensure that your overarching life goals are congruent with your long-term objectives. Take a moment to reflect upon your aspirations and contemplate the goals you aim to accomplish within the foreseeable future, as well as

envisioning the ideal manifestation of your life. Take into account your principles, interests, and aspirations for the future.

2. Ensure the specificity of your objectives: Upon defining your vision, it is imperative to make your long-term objectives specific. They ought to be unambiguous, quantifiable, and attainable. Rather than establishing an ambiguous goal such as 'achieve success,' establish a precise objective such as 'attain a promotion to a managerial role within a timeframe of five years.'

3. Harmonize your goals with your principles: Guarantee that your enduring aspirations are in accord with your individual values. Should your objectives be in conflict with your values, you might encounter challenges in sustaining

your motivation and steadfastness towards their attainment.

4. Segment your objectives into incremental milestones: Segmenting your overarching objectives into smaller, attainable milestones can enhance their attainability and serve as a driving force for sustained motivation. Please ascertain the precise measures required to accomplish each objective, and establish deadlines for each individual measure.

5. Keep track of your progress: Continuously evaluate your advancements towards your overarching goals. Monitor your accomplishments and make necessary modifications to your objectives. Commend your triumphs and glean wisdom from your failures. Exhibit adaptability: Demonstrate a willingness to modify your overarching goals in

response to shifting priorities and changing circumstances. The course of life is subject to constant change, necessitating the adjustment of one's goals to accommodate unforeseen circumstances or potential avenues for growth.

In summary, the act of delineating long-term objectives constitutes a vital component in establishing purposeful aspirations and efficiently administering one's time. By delineating your vision, rendering your objectives tangible, harmonizing them with your core principles, disassembling them into smaller milestones, scrutinizing your advancement, and adapting as needed, you can establish a foundation for triumph and ultimately attain your desired results.

Drawbacks of Remote Work

Frequently, it proves more effortless to ascertain the benefits associated with remote work as opposed to contemplating the drawbacks. Nevertheless, by gaining a deeper comprehension of these drawbacks, you will enhance your ability to effectively acclimate to the remote work environment. This is because it will allow you to identify the areas in which improvement is needed.

Distractions

It can be challenging to maintain focus while operating in a remote work environment. Occasionally, family members can unintentionally be a source of significant distractions. Your significant other could potentially request your assistance, the children may inquire about your activities, or your pets may seek your attention. Furthermore, in addition to the aforementioned factors, it is imperative to acknowledge that while situated in the confines of one's own dwelling, individuals are inevitably confronted with various other enticements that must be discerned and resisted. The presence of television, online shopping, and deliveries can readily divert you from your work in the absence of supervision. The concept of having the television functioning as background noise during work is inherently flawed, as it will inevitably lead to distraction.

Lack of Social Interactions

Occasionally, the experience of working remotely may elicit feelings of solitude. In the event that you reside in solitude and your abode maintains an environment of tranquility during your work hours, you might encounter challenges in sustaining your concentration. Furthermore, it is not uncommon to begin experiencing a sense of longing for the presence of one's coworkers in the workplace. Despite ongoing communication, the experience of interacting with individuals in person yields a distinguishable contrast. This has the potential to impact your psychological well-being and shape your perspective towards remote work.

Security Concerns

Contingent upon the nature of your professional occupation, you may harbor apprehensions concerning the mode of document dissemination during remote work situations. While advancements in technology have unquestionably facilitated enhanced connectivity, they have concurrently exposed us to the vulnerabilities associated with cybercrime. Hence, should your company fail to adequately attend to your concerns, you may be inclined to refrain from remote work and experience a greater sense of ease in returning to the workplace.

Lack of Office Equipment

Working remotely without the appropriate resources in place can present a considerable obstacle. It is not within the means of every individual to procure a home office comprising of devices such as printers, expansive computer screens, ergonomically designed chairs, and keyboards. While it may initially be possible to enjoy the convenience of working on your couch for a day or two, over the course of several weeks, you will inevitably begin to experience discomfort in your back, thereby reinforcing your preference for the ergonomic qualities of your office chair.

Self-Regulation

Not all individuals possess the capacity to operate effectively in solitude. Engaging in remote work entails assuming responsibility for one's working schedule and tasks performed during that designated period. This task is frequently more conveniently expressed than executed. There is no need for a reminder to engage in work within a professional office environment. It is imperative that you are aware of the necessity to do so. Nonetheless, while in the confines of your domicile, it becomes imperative to effectively manage and utilize your time.

Lack of Motivation

In the absence of face-to-face interactions with your team or manager, you may experience a decrease in motivation. Frequently, individuals fail to comprehend the extent of the encouragement they receive within the professional sphere until its absence becomes apparent. "When colleagues observThis task becomes more challenging in situations where all individuals are telecommuting. Concealing one's hardships becomes more feasible when maintaining a distance, thereby impeding the potential assistance of others. Acquiring and honing self-motivation skills can prove beneficial, yet the efficacy of such efforts can often pale in comparison to the impact of receiving encouragement from external sources. This is the point at which communication becomes crucial.

Enhance the amount of meaningful time spent with your child as a means of demonstrating affection.

It is of utmost importance as a single mother to guarantee that your child experiences a sense of love and security in the support you provide. Demonstrating your fondness through verbal assertions, deeds, and the generous allocation of your time is imperative for their psychological welfare.

Presented below are a selection of impactful methods to showcase your affection and fortify the connection between you and your partner:

● Incorporate daily positive statements: Establish the practice of consistently reinforcing positive beliefs in your child. Recognize and commenurate their endeavors and accomplishments, irrespective of their magnitude, and present sincere admiration. Not only does this enhance their self-esteem, but it also serves to underscore the notion that you hold their uniqueness in high regard and actively commemorate it.

● Participate in recreational activities: Dedicate valuable leisure time to engaging in activities with your child, as it can provide profound insights. Through engaging in play, one is able to acquire perceptiveness regarding their individuality, inclinations, and predilections. It presents an occasion to establish rapport with them, nurturing a feeling of confidence and camaraderie.

● Collaborative reading session: Engaging in shared reading offers a potent avenue to delve into the profound realm of your child's thoughts and feelings. It fosters discourse and provides opportunities for them to express their perspectives and emotions. Furthermore, it fosters a passion for acquiring knowledge and can evolve into a treasured habit.

● **Emphasize the importance of spending quality time:** Purposefully dedicating time to your child communicates a distinct message that they occupy a significant role in your life. Whether it entails partaking in their preferred pursuits, engaging in sincere dialogues, or merely being present during routine occurrences, your presence serves to affirm your steadfast dedication to them.

Ensure effective communication channels are established and maintained with your children.

As a single mother, it can be demanding to handle the expectations or solicitations of your children, as what may appear to be a reasonable request at one point in time may become unfeasible on another occasion. Acknowledging your constraints concerning time and resources is imperative, and expressing these limitations assertively is entirely appropriate.

Rather than suppressing your feelings of frustration or withholding the motives underlying your choices, it is advisable to adopt a transparent and candid approach with your children. Elucidate the parameters or restrictions that govern your reactions to their solicitations. When children are approached with maturity and honesty, they possess the capacity to comprehend and employ reasoning.

Through transparent communication, you not only articulate the significance of establishing limits but also impart a valuable life lesson to your children. They have the ability to acquire respect for limitations and cultivate their capacity for logical reasoning through the observation of your conduct.

Effective communication nurtures trust and promotes comprehension within the familial unit. Children acquire an understanding of the significance of observing personal limits and cultivate discernment in making responsible choices.

By exemplifying effective communication and boundary establishment, you become a valuable role model for your children, imparting vital life skills to them.

It is imperative for a single mother to uphold effective communication with her children and establish distinct limits. Being forthright about your constraints facilitates the cultivation of logical reasoning and the fostering of reverence towards limits in your offspring.

In conclusion, these actions ultimately foster improved familial dynamics, decreased levels of stress, and heightened efficacy for both parents and their children.


Procedural Guidelines for Implementing the Pomodoro Technique

The Pomodoro Technique is a time management strategy innovated by Francesco Cirillo during the 1980s, premised upon the notion that undisturbed periods of dedicated work yield optimal results.

In order to execute the Pomodoro technique, a timer will be required. Whilst the nomenclature of this methodology originates from the culinary tomato (Pomodoro in Italian) that Cirillo employed during his academic ventures, it is not imperative to strictly adhere to such a tool. Currently, timers of various kinds are easily accessible, extending to an extensive range of digital applications tailored to serve this purpose.

To commence the application of this technique, adhere to the following sequence of actions:

1. Task designation: Elect a task of your preference, encompassing both professional and academic pursuits. This assignment ought to be of a significant scale that necessitates focused attention, yet it should not be of such magnitude as to become excessively burdensome.

2. Establishing the duration: Set the timer to a time interval of 25 minutes.

Such time intervals are commonly referred to as 'pomodoros'. The primary objective is to dedicate undisturbed focus to your homework within these time frames.

3. Engage in homework tasks: Initiate the process of working on your homework. In the event of being sidetracked by an idea or auxiliary task, it is advisable to record such distractions on a piece of paper for future reference while redirecting your attention towards the primary task at hand.

4. Conclusion of the tomato: Once the allotted time has elapsed, take a brief break and record on a sheet of paper that a Pomodoro has been accomplished. The action of delineating each finished Pomodoro will provide you with a feeling of fulfillment.

5. Interim respite: It is imperative to observe a five minute interval following every Pomodoro. This short respite facilitates cognitive processing and aids in the assimilation of information, thereby enhancing preparation for the subsequent Pomodoro session.

6. Extended break: It is advisable to allocate a period of time ranging between 15 to 30 minutes for recuperation upon accomplishing four successive Pomodoros. This extended period of rest facilitates the restoration of your cognitive vitality in preparation for subsequent work sessions.

It is imperative that you adhere to the designated timings. If one completes a task prior to the conclusion of the Pomodoro, they may utilize the remaining time to engage in a thorough review of their work or make preparations for the subsequent task. If you are unable to complete the task within a single Pomodoro, there is no need for concern. Continue to devote your efforts to the task during the forthcoming Pomodoro session.

The Pomodoro technique not solely enhances productivity, but also imparts the discipline of effectively managing time rather than opposing it. This methodology possesses a high degree of adaptability that allows for the customization of its application according to your individual requirements, as long as the fundamental principle of alternating periods of intensive work and subsequent periods of rest is upheld.

## Taking A Look At How You Currently Manage Your Time

Self-examination exercises are esteemed instruments for evaluating one's existing time management tendencies and discerning areas in need of enhancement. In the ensuing pages, we shall examine several self-reflection exercises aimed at facilitating an enhanced understanding of your time management skills, delving into more comprehensive analysis of these exercises in subsequent chapters.

Time Journal: Maintain a comprehensive record for a duration of one week or longer, meticulously noting the allocation of your time. Please take note of every single activity, regardless of its magnitude. This will enable you to recognize recurring trends and discern how your time is allocated. One may opt to utilize a physical journal or employ a time-tracking application for this purpose.

Preliminary Assessment: Please outline your present assignments and obligations, encompassing both personal and occupational domains. Allocate a priority level to each item, ranging from high to low. Consider whether your current allocation of time corresponds with these priorities and whether you are dedicating an excessive amount of time to tasks of lesser importance.

Perform a time evaluation: Conduct an analysis of your daily regimen to determine the exact amount of time allocated to different activities. Classify them according to professional duties, personal engagements, recreational pursuits, and unproductive diversions.

This exercise will bring attention to aspects where adjustments can be made.

Objective Alignment: Engage in self-reflection regarding your immediate and future objectives. Does the manner in which you engage in your daily activities and manage your time correspond to the objectives you have set? If that is not the case, contemplate on how you may modify your schedule to more effectively align with your goals.

Weekly Evaluation: Conclude each week by assessing your achievements and reviewing tasks that were left unfinished due to time constraints. Reflect on the reasons behind the incompleteness of specific tasks and consider alternate approaches that could have been employed. This will enable you to derive lessons from your past encounters.

Identify Activities Conducive to Inefficient Use of Time: Compile a comprehensive inventory of prevalent activities or tendencies that result in the wastage of time, encompassing actions such as excessive engagement in social media, prolonged meetings, or maintenance of disorderly work environments. Identifying these productivity inhibitors is the initial action towards their elimination or mitigation.

Energy Fluctuations: Take note of your energy levels throughout the course of the day. Determine the periods during which you are most efficient and attentive, as well as those times when your level of energy tends to decline. Efficiently manage your time by strategically aligning high-priority tasks with your periods of peak energy.

Conduct an evaluation of task delegation and outsourcing possibilities to determine if there are any responsibilities that can be assigned to others or contracted out. Take the time to contemplate whether you possess any challenges in relinquishing control and consider avenues to alleviate your workload.

Effectiveness vs. Efficiency: Take into account whether you prioritize effectiveness (attaining significant outcomes) or efficiency (expeditiously accomplishing tasks). Achieving equilibrium between the two is paramount for ensuring efficient time management.

Requesting Feedback: Request evaluations from reliable colleagues, acquaintances, or mentors concerning your proficiency in time management. They have the potential to offer valuable perspectives and recommendations for enhancement that you may not have taken into account.

Contemplate Time Allocation: Assess if the time you are dedicating is allocated towards pursuits that harmonize with your principles and future objectives. Is an adequate amount of time being allocated towards personal development, nurturing relationships, and attending to self-care needs?

Establish SMART Objectives: Establish clear, quantifiable, attainable, pertinent, and time-limited (SMART) objectives to enhance your time management skills. Consistently evaluate the advancement made towards these objectives.

These self-reflection exercises will facilitate the acquisition of a more precise comprehension regarding your current time management practices, enabling you to identify areas for potential optimization and enhance your efficiency and effectiveness in attaining your objectives. Please bear in mind that cultivating self-awareness serves as the initial stride towards effecting significant transformations in your time management practices.

Adopting a Commitment to Lifelong Learning and Personal Development

Consider Maya, a seasoned marketing specialist who perceives every new endeavor as a chance to enhance her expertise. She proactively pursues educational opportunities, such as courses, workshops, and resources, in order to augment her expertise. Maya epitomizes the essence of lifelong learning – the recognition that intellectual and personal development persists beyond the confines of formal education. Through the cultivation of an insatiable passion for learning, one can proactively position oneself at the forefront of advancements and maintain relevance within a perpetually shifting environment.

Integrating Sustained Development within Your Daily Regimen

Introducing Oliver, an industrious entrepreneur who diligently commits himself to daily deliberate practice. He acknowledges that maintaining a steadfast level of dedication is pivotal to achieving expertise. Oliver's dedication to gradual improvement yields positive results in the long run, regardless of whether he is enhancing his public speaking aptitude or refining his business strategies. Through the deliberate integration of deliberate practice into your daily regimen, you can enhance your aptitudes and attain extraordinary outcomes, gradually and methodically.

Conquering Obstacles through an Optimistic and Resilient Mental Attitude

Approaching life's obstacles with an optimistic and resilient mindset can yield profound transformative effects. Consider the case of Alex, an aspiring entrepreneur, who confronts a multitude of challenges during the initiation of his startup. Instead of allowing setbacks to demoralize him, Alex perceives them as valuable opportunities for growth that propel him towards his objectives. By adopting the mentality of Alex, one can transform challenges into opportunities for progress. Similar to him, you will acquire the ability to embrace challenges, foster resilience, and uncover the strength of maintaining a positive perspective even in the midst of hardship.

View setbacks as chances for personal and professional development.

Regard challenges as opportunities for valuable learning.

Nurture resilience through the maintaining of a positive outlook.

Dear Reader

I am delighted to introduce to you the 7-Day Growth Mindset Transformation Plan, meticulously curated to support you in embarking upon a transformative voyage of self-enhancement and individual development. This meticulously devised plan aims to steer you towards adopting a growth mindset and leveraging your potential to surmount obstacles and attain exceptional achievements. I strongly urge you to not only adopt this plan personally but also to disseminate it among someone in your immediate circles. When two individuals mutually agree to uphold the established plan in collaboration, they forge an exclusive alliance rooted in accountability. By fostering collaboration and encouraging one another, you will cultivate a sense of expediency and responsibility that can result in remarkable metamorphoses. As you engage in these deliberate strides towards personal growth, it is crucial to bear in mind that your expedition encompasses more than just your own advancement. It also entails instigating favorable transformations in the individuals surrounding you.

Warm regards,

William

# 7-Day Program for Cultivating a Growth Mindset

## First Day: Embrace the Shift in Mindset

Commence your expedition by recognizing the influence of a mindset focused on growth.

Contemplate on the aspects of your life in which you have once firmly held predetermined convictions.

Disrupt a well-established belief by recontextualizing it as a chance for personal development.

## Day 2: Addressing and Overcoming Your Obstacles

Please identify a difficult task or obstacle that you have been hesitant to confront as a result of apprehension or lack of confidence.

Divide the challenge into smaller, achievable tasks.

Develop a comprehensive strategy to address these tasks within the upcoming weeks.

Day 3: Embracing the Delight of Continuous Education

Select an area of study or expertise that you have long desired to acquire.

Engage with digital resources, educational courses, or literary materials pertaining to your selected subject matter.

Allocate a designated period ranging from 30 minutes to one hour on a daily basis for the purpose of concentrated study and discovery.

Day 4: Utilize Setbacks as Catalysts for Personal Growth

Reflect on a recent occurrence of adversity or disappointment.

Please record three lessons or insights that you have acquired from the aforementioned experience.

Welcome those lessons as milestones paving the way for personal development and enhancement.

Day 5: Cultivating Resilience

Participate in a physical endeavor or fitness regimen that poses a challenge to you.

In the midst of experiencing physical discomfort, endeavor to reframe the encounter in a positive manner.

Acknowledge the resemblances between physical and mental fortitude.

Day 6: Utilizing Affirmations and Mental Imagery for Positivity

Allocate a brief span of time in the morning to engage in the practice of affirmative self-reflection.

Envision yourself effectively triumphing over a difficulty that you are presently encountering.

During the course of the day, endeavor to summon the cognitive representation in order to augment your self-assurance and drive.

Seventh Day: Contemplation and Advancement

Take a moment to contemplate the experiences, insights, and shifts in perspective that have occurred during the preceding week.

Compose a concise journal entry documenting your personal development journey.

Establish a forward-looking objective for the forthcoming weeks, with dedicated attention towards a particular domain in which you aim to enhance your abilities.

By faithfully adhering to this 7-day regimen, you will make substantial progress in adopting a growth mindset. Please bear in mind that the process of transformation does not occur instantaneously. However, through the persistent cultivation of this mindset, you will observe substantial alterations in your approach to challenges, setbacks, and learning opportunities. The commencement of your endeavor to unleash your complete capabilities has recently commenced, and the consistent dedication to daily practice will greatly contribute to your transformation into an individual committed to personal growth.

Execution and Enhancement of the Timetable:

Crafting an individualized itinerary merely constitutes the initial phase. This section will provide readers with comprehensive guidance on effectively establishing and enhancing their time management system. Strategies to uphold adherence to the proposed schedule, surmount impediments, and implement necessary adaptations will be examined to guarantee sustainable achievement in the long run.

Progressive Execution: Systematically phasing in the new timetable to aid in acclimatization.

Utilizing Reminders and Alarms: Employing the use of reminders and alarms to ensure productivity and efficient time management.

Ensuring Accountability: Fostering support from colleagues or utilizing time management resources to uphold accountability.

Identifying and Resolving Challenges: Acknowledging impediments and devising strategies to remain on track.

Ongoing Evaluation and Adaptation: Continuously assessing the efficiency of the timetable and making appropriate adaptations.

Conclusion:

Creating an individualized approach to managing time is an impactful strategy for optimizing efficiency, attaining objectives, and nurturing a harmonious equilibrium in one's life. Through acknowledging the importance of an individualized timetable, evaluating one's current utilization of time, and employing a meticulously crafted framework, individuals can maximize their time and vitality in order to live lives of gratification and meaning. By prioritizing self-awareness and adaptability, an individually tailored timetable enables individuals to assume authority over their schedules, embrace efficiency, and maximize their daily potential.

Advantages

It fosters enhanced concentration on the task at hand. It serves as a highly effective method to eradicate disturbances and disruptions. It establishes a hierarchy in which the completion of the task assumes utmost significance, while the remaining tasks serve as supplementary components within the allocated time period. It incites a heightened sense of urgency to successfully complete the task within the designated timeframe.

Engaging in less demanding tasks can lead to feelings of boredom, causing our minds to seek diversion through activities such as social media or socializing. However, upon implementing proactive time restrictions or segmenting activities into predefined time frames, these tedious tasks can be effortlessly accomplished within the allocated time.

Moreover, it serves as a means to counter the snares of perfectionism. On occasion, when we exhibit a modicum of creativity or a desire to perform optimally in a given undertaking, we frequently neglect to consider the duration of time devoted to its completion. Our objective is to attain a higher level of excellence by dedicating a significant amount of time within an open timeframe, with the sole purpose of attaining impeccable quality. However, when we consciously allocate a designated end time, we begin harnessing our mental faculties from the very first minute in our pursuit of achieving a state of near-perfection. Ultimately, the foremost priority is ensuring that the objective is accomplished optimally within the allocated timeframe.

• Incorporate an additional time zone if you collaborate with clients or colleagues from different countries.

If your professional interactions encompass international colleagues or clients, incorporating an additional time zone or two into your calendar will greatly facilitate your comprehension of multiple time zones. This feature will enable the display of both your own and your client's working and personal times on your list, thereby promoting clarity and understanding. Experiment with your preferred applications or alternatively, utilize spreadsheet software; by printing the document, you may establish a dual time zone within the designated time column.

# Planning Your Time Wisely For The Day

## The Advantages of Implementing Daily Planning

An effectively organized day commences with strategic planning. Engaging in daily planning guarantees efficient time allocation and adherence to goal attainment. It facilitates the establishment of priorities, formulation of realistic timetables, and adaption to unforeseen adversities.

Every morning or the preceding evening, allocate a few moments to strategically outline your day. Please ascertain your utmost priority tasks and designate specific time periods for their completion. Establishing a strategic framework bestows upon you a sense of purpose and guidance as you embark upon your daily professional endeavors.

Time Blocking

By dedicating focused time to particular tasks, you reduce the likelihood of distractions and multitasking.

For instance, in the case of a pending project report, it would be prudent to assign a dedicated time slot of two hours exclusively for the purpose of working on the aforementioned report. In this duration, it is advised to close email and messaging applications, directing your attention exclusively towards the task at hand.

The practice of time blocking enables individuals to effectively tackle indispensable tasks while avoiding the sensation of being burdened by an interminable roster of obligations.

## To-Do Lists

Agendas are a traditional yet efficient method for organizing and overseeing your everyday responsibilities. Compose a comprehensive list of all tasks that require completion within the day, and proceed to establish a hierarchical order for their execution. As you achieve completion of tasks, mark them as accomplished on your list. Task lists offer a visual depiction of your advancements and aid in safeguarding against the oversight of significant matters.

Aside from your responsibilities at work, it is advisable to incorporate personal obligations and breaks into your daily agenda to sustain a healthy equilibrium between work and personal life.

In the forthcoming chapters, we will delve into strategies aimed at enhancing productivity, surmounting procrastination, and managing distractions; these techniques are designed to assist you in maximizing your scheduled workday.

Prioritization Techniques

Suppose we consider Ariel as having a total of five goals. She is fully aware that they adhere strictly to the principles of SMART, however, there exists a secondary predicament. She is uncertain as to where to commence. Fortunately, prioritization offers a clear-cut solution for us. We will be utilizing Ariel as our next exemplar, who encounters a prevalent issue. As stated by Alec Mackenzie, a multitude of the 'time traps' delineated in his literary work A lack of priorities can give rise to the Time Trap. By perusing the concluding section of the book, wherein the author has thoughtfully provided a concise overview of each trap's underlying factors and corresponding resolutions, I would venture to assert that approximately twenty-five percent of them demonstrate a causal link akin to the absence of proper prioritization.

So, further establishing Ariel. She is enrolled as a Communications major at the Community College where she is currently pursuing her studies. During the summer, she engages in an internship and promptly discovers that her schedule becomes encroached upon. It appears as though she has lost dominion over it. The alignment of priorities appears to be confounded, as her aspirations seem misguided and unattainable. Ariel is in close proximity to regaining control. As per her supervisor's observation, she ought to acquire the skill of effectively prioritizing the unforeseen tasks that arise throughout her day. Therefore, he suggests that she acquaint herself with the identical approach that we are about to undertake: The Eisenhower Matrix.

To address this matter, we shall firstly acquire knowledge of the Eisenhower Matrix. Although the moniker may appear daunting, the strategy itself is relatively straightforward. In accordance with the findings elucidated by Bratterud et al. According to Al (2020), the Eisenhower Decision Matrix, which is attributed to the task management system employed by the US President Dwight Eisenhower, serves as a visual representation employed in the strategic execution and planning of tasks. Visualize a square shape that is partitioned into four distinct sectors. The uppermost segments have been designated for priority assignments. However, the two at the bottom pertain to items of insignificance. We will implement a comparable partition on both the left and right sides. We will allocate our immediate tasks to the left side while placing less time-sensitive tasks in the rightmost section. Henceforth, our square shall be partitioned into distinct quadrants, specifically:

The 'Do' Quadrant is designated for matters of utmost urgency and significance. To clarify, it is imperative that you prioritize tasks that are crucial for your personal or professional well-being as your utmost immediate concern.

Quadrant for 'Scheduling': Situated in the upper-right corner, this quadrant is designated to accommodate significant tasks that are not time-sensitive within the immediate future. Activities that lend themselves well to scheduling on a calendar are highly suitable for this purpose, such as ensuring regular communication with a family member or participating in a symposium focused on a subject of personal interest.

The segment situated at the bottom-left quadrant, referred to as the 'Delegate' quadrant, encompasses tasks that are both time-sensitive and of relatively lower importance. These frequently do not exhibit strong alignment with your set of skills or values. However, they must still be managed expeditiously and effectively. To resolve these concerns, it is advisable to recommend an individual who possesses more suitable qualifications for the given task or to empower the person who possesses the utmost competence and proficiency by equipping them with the necessary tools and information.

"Neglected" Quadrant: Furthermore, located at the lower right quadrant, we will observe matters that hold no significance or urgency. Frequently, tendencies to procrastinate can be categorized within this framework. Furthermore, as straightforward as it may appear, one should refrain from participating in such activities.

Continuing the discussion on Ariel as an exemplar, her objectives afford her the ability to ascertain the course of action for each task in her daily routine. She designates three as having high priority and significance, while categorizing seven as significant but not requiring immediate attention. In addition, she encountered several insignificant yet time-sensitive responsibilities throughout the course of the day, which she effectively assigned to suitable colleagues. Although none of her objectives aligned with the final category, she had to resist the inclination to peruse abbreviated content on social media platforms. In conclusion, she could employ the Eisenhower Matrix to enhance her daily clarity. Commendable progress for a beginning!

The Pareto Principle represents an additional potent resource within our reach. Similar to our approach with the Eisenhower Matrix, it provides us with a more distinct comprehension of the tasks that require immediate attention and those that can be postponed. According to a medical article published in 2018, it has been identified that a limited set of factors significantly influence the outcome of a situation. Recognizing this, the authors decided to utilize the Pareto chart technique in order to pinpoint the specific areas that required their attention. As anticipated, a sole determinant accounted for a significant majority of the complications encountered within their workflow, comprising 78% of the total issues.

The Pareto Principle can be considered an approximate heuristic. Specifically, the cause of 80% of a certain outcome can be attributed to only 20% of the contributing factors. This principle also extends to the domain of Time management: Allocating the optimal 20% of our effort will yield 80% of the desired outcome for a given task. Regrettably, the opposite holds true as well, indicating that approximately 80% of our efforts will be allocated to achieving the final 20% of refinement.

Nevertheless, the primary objective of this principle lies in the act of prioritization. You demonstrate exceptional aptitude in specific domains, which remains applicable both within and beyond professional contexts. Utilizing your expertise in the field, discern tasks of significant importance, particularly within time-sensitive projects, and concentrate your efforts on these. You will discover that this significantly improves the efficiency of your job, enabling a greater number of resolved items to be achieved.

Both approaches result in a vague understanding of how to handle non-urgent yet critical assignments. Paradoxically, the majority of seasoned professionals prioritize their Scheduling quadrant by allocating the highest number of tasks. A portion of this can be attributed to crises, which often entail unforeseen and pressing obligations. Furthermore, it is congruent with the initial concept underlying the Eisenhower Matrix. The inventor who holds official recognition and who has formerly served as president made the statement, "The matters deserving utmost attention are rarely immediately pressing, while the matters requiring immediate attention are rarely of utmost significance."

## CHAPTER 3

### TIME TRACKING AND EXAMINATION

Proposed course of action: Maintain a journal documenting your daily activities over a period of one week, and subsequently evaluate the allocation of your time.

Time holds immense value in the relentless pace of modern society. Gaining insight into your time allocation is vital in enhancing your efficiency and attaining your goals, irrespective of whether you are a busy professional, an entrepreneur, or a student. The ebook titled "A Comprehensive Guide to Time Tracking and Analysis" will provide step-by-step instructions on documenting your daily tasks over a period of one week, enabling you to assess the collected data effectively. Upon the completion of this endeavor, you will acquire the necessary skills and knowledge to optimize each and every moment.

Time Management\\\'s Power

Analyze the factors that contribute to the necessity of effective time management for achieving success.

Discover the potential benefits that may arise from the strategic evaluation and examination of one's time utilization and allocation.

Establishing Your Time Monitoring System Gain knowledge on effectively tracking your time through a range of tools and methodologies, encompassing both traditional pen-and-paper notebooks and modern digital applications.

Acquire the knowledge on constructing your own time tracking system through a comprehensive guide comprising of sequential instructions.

The Difficulties Encountered in Weekly Time Monitoring

Commence a challenge spanning the course of one week with the purpose of diligently recording and documenting your daily undertakings.

Acquire techniques for maintaining accuracy and uniformity throughout the week.

## Investigating Your Time Logs

Commence the procedure of meticulously reviewing and categorizing your records of time allocation.

Examine patterns and areas with potential for enhancement.

## Time-Boosters and Time-Stealers

Discover effective strategies to mitigate customary non-productive actions.

Explore strategies for optimizing your peak productivity periods.

## Personal Action Plan Creation

Develop a distinctive course of action by drawing upon the findings of your time analysis.

Formulate SMART (Specific, Measurable, Achievable, Relevant, Time-Bound) objectives with the aim of enhancing your proficiency in time management.

Implementing Long-Term Changes

Learn the proper method of integrating your action plan into your routine endeavors.

Overcome common barriers and uphold unwavering commitment to your pursuit of effective time management.

Assessing Outcomes and Modifying Course

Acquire the knowledge and skills to assess your progress over a period of time.

As your proficiency in managing time progresses, adapt your methodologies accordingly.

Illustrative Instances of Achievement and Analytical Examinations

Derive inspiration from real-life examples of individuals who enhanced the quality of their lives through effective utilization of time.

Strategies for Sustaining Optimal Time Management Practices

Acquire the skills necessary to efficiently organize and handle your time, while sustaining your drive and determination.

Research innovative time management strategies for ongoing achievement.

The Impact of Delegation and Team Management on Effective Time Management

The efficient allocation of duties is a crucial component in effectively managing time for entrepreneurs. Through the delegation of responsibilities to your team members, you can offload certain tasks and focus more attention on prioritizing complex duties that require specialized attention. Efficient delegation necessitates meticulous strategic planning and thoughtful consideration to ensure the appropriate assignment of tasks, thereby ensuring successful and elevated execution of said tasks.

Effective team management is essential in optimizing productivity and attaining organizational objectives. As the owner, it is imperative for you to effectively guide and inspire your team, fostering an environment wherein they can reach the pinnacle of their capabilities. This pertains to establishing explicit expectations, delivering constructive feedback and assistance, and acknowledging and incentivizing their achievements.

Wrapping up

Within this chapter, we have explored the significance of time management in the realm of entrepreneurship, as well as the pivotal role that delegation and team management play in optimizing productivity and attaining predetermined business objectives. By efficiently organizing your daily tasks and assigning them to your team members, you can free yourself from the limitations posed by time. This will enable a greater emphasis on strategic decision-making, leading to increased efficiency in output production and enhancing profitability margins at the same time.

Exercise: Identify Assignments to Entrust to Others

Assigning tasks is an essential aspect of proficient time management. As an entrepreneur, it is critical to discern the tasks that can be assigned to fellow team members. Through the efficient delegation of tasks, you can allocate more time to concentrate on essential operations within the business.

• Compile a comprehensive inventory of the routine tasks and responsibilities implicated by your business operations.

• Evaluate each task to determine whether it is exclusive to your role or if it can be assigned to a member within your team.

• Determine the team member who possesses the highest level of qualification to assume each task that can be assigned responsibilities.

• Schedule a meeting with the aforementioned team member for the purpose of reviewing the tasks at hand and delineating precise guidelines and expectations.

- Supervise the advancement of the designated task and provide constructive feedback and support when necessary.

Through effective delegation of tasks, individuals can optimize their time allocation towards crucial company endeavors, resulting in enhanced productivity across the organization.

## Establishing Favorable Patterns OfBehavior

Putting the Power of Habits to Work Our daily routines have a significant impact on our lives. While good habits provide us the capacity to do what we set out to do, bad habits can slow or even stop our forward movement.

Getting Rid of Unhealthy Patterns:

It is possible to break free of habits, despite the fact that it can be difficult. Please follow these directions as closely as possible:

Be conscious of your routines: Recognizing the patterns that you want to break is the first step in the process of doing so. What kinds of actions do you take that are bad for your health?

Determine what causes them to react: After you've recognized your patterns of behavior, the next step is to figure out what causes them to manifest themselves. What are the motivating factors that drive you to engage in these behaviors?

Figure out your routines: Once you have an understanding of the triggers, you should look for alternative actions or routines that can take the place of the habit.

Make a game plan that includes the following: With a routine in mind, devise a plan for putting it into action and adhering to it regularly. This can be done by designating certain time periods or by incorporating it into your daily calendar.

Keep moving forward: The ability to break undesirable behaviors takes time, effort, and patience. If you make a mistake, don't let it discourage you. You should just give it another go.

How to Begin the Process of Developing Positive Habits and How to Get Started with Positive Habits.

Developing new routines can be difficult at first. It is not in any way impossible to do so. The following is a list of steps that you can follow:

To begin, let's consider something: It's best not to try to make too many changes at once. Instead, zero down on a single routine that you wish to become part of your routine.

Don't let it get out of hand: Make it as simple and uncomplicated as possible to include your habit in your daily activities. This could involve deciding on a time and location, or pledging to put in the necessary practice. The key to success is consistency: The key to successfully building habits is to continue to engage in those behaviors even when you do not feel particularly motivated or enthusiastic about doing so.

Reward yourself along the way: Whenever you successfully engage in your habit, offer yourself a reward. This will encourage you to continue doing what you need to do. Consider this an incentive for making consistent progress and staying motivated.

Developing habits takes time and work; instant changes may not be obvious right away, but don't allow that discourage you from persisting in your efforts. Persevere despite challenges: Developing habits involves time and effort.

Why Should You Go on Short Vacations More Often?

The warm weather of summer is just around the corner. As a result, a significant number of us are currently devoting the majority of our waking hours to gathering information regarding exciting new locations to visit during our long overdue holiday. However, it might be challenging to reserve a significant portion of one's schedule for a lengthy trip.

Going on a shorter vacation, or a "mini-vacation," is one method to alleviate some of the strain that comes with planning and preparing for longer trips. Taking off Friday and Monday in order to have a long four-day weekend is what's meant by the term "mini-vacation." This provides sufficient time for much-needed recuperation as well as the opportunity to travel to a different city or region.

A recent survey found that only 51% of working Americans take advantage of their available paid vacation time. People continue to work despite the mounting tension because they are afraid that their jobs will be eliminated. But isn't this going to cause more problems than it solves?

Here are some compelling arguments in favor of the concept of the weekend getaway.

Recharges the battery

We let excitement into our lives when we do things like go somewhere new and different or attempt new activities. This excitement gives us a boost to our energy levels and carries over to when we return back to our homes. It's possible that going on a short vacation or getting away for the weekend is exactly what we need to re-energize ourselves so that we can perform better at work.

### Resets one's mental state

When we are overburdened with never-ending to-do lists, continual calendar reminders, and expectations as well as distractions tugging us in every direction, life can feel as though it is spinning out of control. When we give our minds a break from the pressures of daily life, it enables us to reset and refocus on what really matters in our lives.

### Recognizes the value of labor

It can feel like a punishment with very little to no payoff if you have to stay late at work to meet a deadline or if you make it a practice to bring work home with you on a regular basis. We have the ability to recognize and appreciate all of the effort that we put in on a daily basis by giving ourselves a reward in the form of a short vacation. Take a break, put away your mobile devices, power down your computer, and disconnect from your email. Permit yourself to enjoy this time as a reward for all of the hard work that has been accomplished.

Reconstitutes objectives

We place a significant amount of value on giving careful consideration to our plans and objectives. You might use the time you have during a short trip to set out your objectives and the steps you need to take to achieve them. This assists in realigning what we feel should be our primary focus. Be precise and set at least one objective for every aspect of your life, including the areas of your physical health, your financial situation, your mental well-being, and your spiritual connection.

Restores one to their youth

Typical business activities, such as attending meetings, working on projects, and striving to meet deadlines, tend to drive people into a mindset that prioritizes work and inhibits recreation. Mini vacations provide us with the opportunity to kick back, relax, and enjoy ourselves in a new environment. Release that part of yourself that has been begging to go for a bike ride, get some ice cream, and spend the day exploring new places. That child should be allowed to run free.

Helps to alleviate tension

It will be helpful in reducing the stress in your life if you can get away from the never-ending emails and phone calls. Stress is a major contributor to both obesity and a wide range of conditions that might threaten one's life. Make the most of your time by going to have a massage, participating in some yoga courses, going on a meditation expedition, or checking out the local attractions. Get away from your stressful circumstances and make good use of the time off by scheduling a trip.

Rearrange your priorities.

Making the priorities of other people our own is a common yet easy mistake to make. Thinking about what really matters enables the mind to zero in on the process of reorganizing one's personal priorities while on the short vacation. Create a fresh list of the things that are significant, and then devise a strategy for turning that list into a reality.

reconnects with friends and family.

Spending time away from your regular routine with loved ones, such as on vacation, might help you feel more connected to those people. Mini trips provide the ideal setting for cultivating those important relationships. Encourage in-depth conversations, times of quiet reflection, and opportunities to simply take pleasure in one other's company.

Although there will always be work to do and little time to accomplish it, you shouldn't forego your paid vacation time just because there will always be work to do. The best organizations can function normally even for a few days without their employees. Therefore, leave your comfort zone and go out into the world to gain some life experience. The advantages of going on vacation greatly outweigh the advantages of working at a desk all day.

## Dull Work And Activities With A Low Priority

Have you ever found yourself investing excessive amounts of time into tasks of minimal significance? It is possible that you have dedicated an entire day to mundane tasks or low-priority assignments, only to come to the realization that by the end of the day, no significant advancement has been made towards your most crucial projects. If that is indeed the case, rest assured that you are not the only one.

In the contemporary era, we are frequently overwhelmed by a multitude of tasks and lists of things to accomplish. One can easily become entangled in minor details and fixate on matters of lesser significance, thereby overlooking critical tasks that will effectively advance our objectives. It is crucial to acknowledge the distinction between mundane tasks and tasks of utmost importance, thereby acquiring the skill of efficient time management.

To address the issue of busywork, the initial step lies in its identification. Carefully examine your agenda and contemplate which tasks hold significant relevance and which ones do not. Are there any tasks within your agenda that could be assigned to another party or potentially removed from consideration? Are there tasks that you are undertaking primarily due to their simplicity or familiarity, rather than their significance or importance?

Upon having determined your tasks of lesser importance, it is now imperative to establish the order of precedence for your most crucial tasks. Take into consideration which tasks hold the utmost significance in the pursuit of your long-term objectives. Which tasks are most likely to have a significant influence on your business, professional trajectory, or personal circumstances? Please direct your attention to these tasks.

It is imperative to acknowledge that tasks of high priority are not necessarily synonymous with those that require immediate attention. The presence of time-sensitive responsibilities may frequently divert our attention from our paramount tasks. This is the reason why acquiring the skill of prioritization is of utmost significance, enabling individuals to concentrate their efforts on the tasks that are most consequential to their overall well-being.

An effective method for giving precedence to your high-priority tasks involves utilizing the Eisenhower Matrix. This straightforward instrument can assist you in discerning between tasks of immediate significance and those of utmost importance, facilitating effective prioritization. The matrix has been partitioned into four distinct quadrants:

Critical and Time-Sensitive: These tasks hold significant importance and require immediate attention.

Of significant importance, yet not requiring immediate attention: These tasks hold significant importance, although they do not necessitate immediate action. They ought to be promptly scheduled and carried out.

Of lesser significance yet requiring immediate attention: These tasks warrant prompt action, although their significance is relatively low. They can frequently be assigned or eradicated.

Insignificant and non-critical: These tasks hold no level of urgency or significance. They should be eliminated.

By employing the Eisenhower Matrix as a means of prioritization, individuals can direct their attention towards tasks of paramount significance, while effectively discarding or allocating tasks that lack inherent importance.

An alternative solution to addressing the issue of excessive workload is to establish a structured timetable and consistent regimen. Allocate dedicated time slots throughout the day or week for critical tasks, adhering to this timetable to the best of your ability. This will assist you in circumventing any potential distractions and maintaining an unwavering focus on your utmost critical tasks.

To sum up, engaging in unproductive tasks and low-priority responsibilities can substantially impede our progress towards achieving our objectives and leading gratifying existences. By discerning our demanding work duties, prioritizing our crucial tasks, and implementing well-defined schedules and routines, we can attain mastery over our time and allocate resources towards our forthcoming undertakings. Please be mindful that time is valuable, and any moment squandered is irreversible.

Myth 4: Efficiency Arises from the Duration of Work Hours

In defiance of prevailing notions, productivity is not contingent upon the quantity of hours devoted to one's desk or a particular occupational role. Indeed, employees frequently demonstrate enhanced efficiency when operating within a conducive environment that nurtures creativity and empowers decision-making. Provided employees possess a clear comprehension of their duties, their ability to yield outcomes remains unaffected by the duration allocated to task completion. In the end, the most crucial aspect lies in their final results.

Myth 5: Direct Physical Contact is Indispensable for Establishing Interpersonal Bonds

While remote work may eradicate face-to-face interactions, employees are still able to establish robust bonds with their coworkers. Virtual communication tools facilitate the interaction, collaboration, and cultivation of personal connections among colleagues. The dynamics of these relationships may vary in comparison to in-person interactions;

nevertheless, their significance remains intact.

## Myth 6: The Erosion of Company Culture in the Context of Remote Work

Numerous employers apprehend that remote work possesses the potential to undermine their organizational culture. Although it is indeed accurate that remote employees do not have physical exposure to mottos, artifacts, or spaces emblematic of a company's values, the quintessence of company culture resides within its personnel and means of communication. Employers have the capacity to sustain a robust organizational culture that surpasses geographical limitations through the strategic transmission of core values and explicit performance standards.

## Myth 7: The Upkeep Costs of Remote Work are Significant

Numerous corporations have discovered that remote work offers substantial cost reductions. Conventional workplace environments necessitate significant expenditure in terms of rental fees, utilities, upkeep, and equipment investments. On the other hand, remote work predominantly depends on digital tools and resources, the majority of which are freely available or affordable. This arrangement has the potential to offer a significantly lower cost burden compared to the expenses associated with maintaining a traditional brick-and-mortar office.

Falsehood 8: Remote Work Causes Social Isolation

Although the shift to remote work may induce sentiments of solitude among certain individuals, it is essential to bear in mind that remote work does not entail seclusion. Employees have the option to accommodate their work routine by utilizing public venues such as coffee shops or maintaining communication with colleagues through virtual collaboration tools. Remote work grants individuals the opportunity to select a conducive and advantageous work setting, thereby affording them flexibility.

Misconception 9: Effectively overseeing a geographically dispersed team is an insurmountable challenge.

It is feasible to effectively oversee a team that is geographically dispersed. By employing appropriate resources and employing effective communication techniques, managers can efficiently supervise their staff and uphold productivity levels. Establishing and cultivating trust, as well as actively offering support and motivation, are imperative in facilitating a flourishing remote work environment. When employees perceive that they are trusted and esteemed, they are inclined to sustain a high level of dedication and commitment towards their professional responsibilities.

How to Implement These Principles and Strategies in Various Aspects of Your Life

These guiding principles and effective strategies have versatile applications across various aspects of your life, encompassing professional endeavors, academic pursuits, domestic routines, personal well-being, leisurely pursuits, and more. Nevertheless, it may be necessary to modify them in accordance with your individual requirements, personal inclinations, or particular situations. Outlined below are several instances wherein these principles and strategies may be effectively implemented across various domains of your existence:

● Employment: You have the ability to establish clear and specific objectives for your assignments or duties, arrange them in order of significance and time sensitivity, anticipate and prepare for any required submission or gatherings, assign or procure assistance from your colleagues or external associates, consolidate or mechanize certain correspondence or documents, and eradicate any sources of disruption within your workspace or internet usage.

● Analysis: It is possible to establish SMART objectives for your courses or assignments, assign them priority based on their level of difficulty and submission date, strategize in advance for your examinations or presentations, allocate some of your research or editing tasks to your peers or instructors, streamline or automate certain aspects of note-taking or revision, and eliminate any potential disturbances while studying in the library or using your laptop.

● Residence: It is possible to establish intelligent objectives for your domestic responsibilities or errands, prioritize them based on their urgency and regularity, anticipate your meals or shopping, assign some of your cleaning or laundry tasks to your family members or professional services, organize and streamline your bill payments or subscription procedures, and minimize interruptions from your television or mobile device.

● Health: It is possible to establish SMART objectives for your physical fitness or well-being, organize them based on their advantages and enjoyment, premeditate your workout routines or appointments, allocate certain cooking or tracking tasks to friends or applications, streamline and automate the process of managing supplements or reminders, and remove any potential distractions originating from the couch or snacks.

● Interests and Pursuits: It is advantageous to establish SMART objectives for your interests or passions, arrange them in order of enjoyment and satisfaction, proactively prepare for your sessions or engagements, entrust aspects of your preparation or equipment to mentors or clubs, consolidate or mechanize certain aspects of your learning or practice, and remove any distractions from your professional or familial responsibilities.

# The Importance Of Self-Control And Perseverance In The Process Of Habit Formation

Although techniques for time management can be helpful, the best way to take use of their full potential is to integrate them into one's daily routine. Discipline and perseverance are two factors that become extremely important at this point in the process. In this part of the discussion, we will look deeper into the significance of these characteristics in the process of forming long-lasting habits as well as how they contribute to the efficiency of time management.

The capacity to exercise mental and behavioral control in order to conform to predetermined expectations or realize predetermined objectives is the essence of discipline. When discussing the management of one's time, the term "discipline" refers to the capacity to adhere to a predetermined schedule or plan, despite the presence of potential interruptions or temptations that could cause one to veer off course. It is the pillar upon which any habit is built and rests. Without discipline, it would be incredibly impossible to keep to any type of routine or structure, and our techniques for time management would be susceptible to failure at the hands of even the smallest obstacle.

On the other hand, the quality of being regular and stable in our attempts to accomplish our goals and duties is what we refer to when we talk about consistency. Our routines can only be maintained by one thing: consistency. Without consistency, we could have days in which we adhere to our plans, followed by days in which we entirely disregard our tactics for managing our time. The ability to maintain our efforts, even on days when the going is rough, is absolutely necessary for the formation of habits that will persist, and consistency gives us that ability.

It is essential to have the understanding that self-control and consistency are not traits that one either possesses or does not possess, but rather are competencies that can be developed via practice over time. To become proficient at something takes time and effort, just like learning any other ability. When it comes to effective time management, one of the most important things to do is to develop good habits.

The process of turning an activity or behavior into a habit requires incorporating it into our typical routine to the point that it becomes practically second nature to carry it out. Because they lessen the number of choices that are presented to us during the day, habits enable us to conserve the mental energy that would otherwise be expended on decision-making. This is especially helpful in terms of time management since it frees up our attention so that we may concentrate on activities that are either more important or more complex.

The process of developing new routines is one that takes a certain amount of time. Discipline and perseverance are necessary components of this process. Maintaining adherence to our ideas for time management can initially be a difficult task. However, if we are self-disciplined and persistent, we will gradually begin to observe how these methods become an organic part of our daily routine.

There are a few different approaches that we can take in order to develop habits that are disciplined and consistent with who we are as individuals. To begin, rather of beginning with major shifts, we can get started with more incremental shifts. For instance, if our objective is to be more efficient with the use of our time, we may begin by devoting only ten minutes every day to the planning of our responsibilities. As we get better at doing this one simple thing on a consistent basis, we'll be able to gradually extend the amount of time we spend making plans.

Second, we can assist ourselves in remaining on track by setting reminders or alarms for ourselves. These nudges can be as straightforward as an alarm set on our phone or a post-it note placed on our workspace. The fact that they offer us with a constant visual reminder of our commitment to effective time management is the most significant thing about them.

Last but not least, it is essential that we treat ourselves with kindness during this process. It is inevitable that there will be times when we deviate from our plans; however, the most essential thing is to avoid being disheartened and to return to our routines as soon as we possibly can. Discipline and consistency do not imply that we must be perfect; rather, they require that we continually push ourselves and remain on track, despite the fact that things may get challenging.

In a nutshell, the building of habits in relation to time management requires a significant amount of discipline as well as perseverance. These abilities enable us to adapt our ideas for time management into long-lasting habits that can boost our productivity and reduce our stress levels via consistent practice and perseverance. We have the ability to make time management a fundamental and second nature component of our life if we are disciplined and consistent.

## Effective Means Of Working Together And Communicating

Facilitate effective communication and foster attentive listening. The achievement of successful teamwork and efficient time management is contingent upon the establishment of effective communication. Participate in active listening, wherein one demonstrates focused attentiveness and comprehensive understanding of others' verbal expressions. In order to promote effective communication, it is advised to abstain from interrupting and instead make an effort to seek clarification and restate information in your own words. Employ appropriate channels and mediums to effectively convey information with clarity and conciseness. It is crucial to exercise caution regarding one's tone and body language as they play a significant role in influencing the perception of one's communication by others. You have the ability to diminish misunderstandings and promote

Facilitating efficient collaboration through the promotion of attentive listening and transparent communication.Employing electronic means for virtual communication.

Virtual communication plays a vital role in modern workplaces that are increasingly characterized by digitalization and geographical separation. Utilize technological platforms and tools to facilitate and enhance communication and collaboration. Whenever feasible, utilize video conferencing as a means to establish camaraderie and strengthen interpersonal bonds during in-person interactions. Utilize messaging applications and project management software to facilitate information exchange and uphold immediate communication. In order to ensure effective and efficient collaboration, it is imperative to establish unambiguous regulations and anticipated norms for online communication. By harnessing the power of technology-enabled virtual communication, you have the opportunity to transcend the constraints imposed by geography and significantly enhance productivity.

It is crucial to set deadlines and define expectations in order to ensure effective time management and promote collaborative efforts.

clear expectations and timelines. It is imperative that project objectives, outputs, and timelines are effectively communicated to every member of the team. Ensure that all individuals are cognizant of their respective responsibilities. Collaboratively determine mutually acceptable timelines, taking into consideration the availability and workload of team members. Provide regular status updates and address any challenges or obstacles that may arise. Establishing clear expectations and implementing designated timeframes facilitates the development of a well-structured approach to collaborative efforts, ensuring timely completion of projects.

Dispensing constructive feedback and fostering a harmonious work environment significantly influence the efficacy of teamwork and communication. Provide your colleagues with constructive feedback, focusing on specific actions and outcomes. Exercise deliberate thought in the selection of your words and generate strategies to elevate your language. Foster a work environment that promotes the recognition and acceptance of suggestions. Celebrate

## 2 The Eisenhower Matrix: Distinguishing Between Urgency and Importance Important

The Eisenhower Matrix, alternatively referred to as the Urgent-Important Matrix, serves as a time management instrument facilitating the prioritization of tasks by considering both their level of urgency and significance. The matrix derives its name from the 34th President of the United States, Dwight D. Eisenhower, renowned for his statement, \\\"Rarely are urgent matters significant, and rarely are significant matters urgent.\\\" This principle aids in discerning between tasks necessitating immediate attention and those that align with your long-term objectives and principles.

The matrix comprises four quadrants:" "The matrix is composed of four quadrants:" "The matrix is made up of four quadrants:" "The matrix encompasses four quadrants:" "The matrix is structured into four quadrants:

1. Quadrant 1: Matters of utmost urgency and significance (Prioritize immediately)

The prompt execution of these tasks is of utmost importance, as they play a pivotal role in achieving your objectives. Instances could consist of unforeseen crises, time constraints, or pressing matters necessitating attention. Please give priority to and promptly finish these tasks.

2. Second Quadrant: Non-urgent yet significant (Scheduling)

The completion of these tasks is crucial in attaining your long-term objectives, yet they do not necessitate prompt action. Illustrations encompass the acts of strategic planning, honing one's expertise, and fostering interpersonal connections. Devote a portion of your schedule to the completion of these tasks, as they play a vital role in your overall progression.

3. Quadrant 3: Pressing yet Nonessential (Delegate)

These tasks necessitate prompt action, yet they do not possess a direct correlation with your objectives. Instances may consist of occurrences such as interruptions, incoming phone calls, or urgent email communications that necessitate an immediate reply. In circumstances where it is feasible, assign these tasks to another individual or discover methods to reduce the amount of time allocated to their completion.

4. Quadrant 4: Lacking urgency and lacking importance (Eliminate)

These tasks lack both urgency and importance, and their completion does not contribute to the achievement of your objectives. Instances encompass trivial pursuits, undue engagement in social media platforms, or unfruitful gatherings. Mitigate or eradicate these tasks to allocate additional time for higher-priority and purposeful assignments.

In order to make use of the Eisenhower Matrix, compile a comprehensive list of your tasks and proceed to assign them to their respective quadrant based on their appropriate classification. Direct your attention towards the timely accomplishment of tasks within Quadrant 1, subsequently allocating dedicated time for the fulfillment of Quadrant 2 tasks. Prioritize the delegation or reduction of time allocated to Quadrant 3 tasks, and strive to eliminate or minimize time devoted to Quadrant 4 tasks. By adhering to this method, you can efficiently allocate priority to your tasks and guarantee that you allocate your time and effort to the endeavors that hold the utmost significance.

B. Reducing interruptions and maintaining concentration

Efficient time management entails the reduction of distractions and maintaining unwavering focus. Numerous diversions may manifest themselves, encompassing notifications on mobile devices, social media platforms, electronic mail, or even the ambient commotion and commotion surrounding your vicinity. Such distractions have the potential to divert your attention from your tasks, impeding your ability to concentrate and effectively carry out your work.

Presented below are a range of methodologies aimed at minimizing distractions and maintaining an unwavering focus.

Establish a designated work area: The establishment of a designated work area, devoid of any potential disruptions, can significantly enhance your concentration and productivity levels. Please ensure that your workspace remains tidy and well-arranged, limiting the presence of only those items necessary for your current task on your desk.

Implement the Pomodoro Technique: The Pomodoro Technique is a reputable methodology of time management that entails allocating a fixed duration – often around 25 minutes – for focused work, subsequently followed by a brief interval of rest. This methodology can aid in maintaining concentration and maximizing one's time.

Disable notifications: Disable notifications on both your mobile device and computer that are unrelated to the current task. This will assist you in circumventing potential distractions caused by extraneous notifications.

Utilize noise-cancellation headphones: When operating within a noisy work setting, employing noise-cancellation headphones can prove highly effective in attenuating disturbances, enabling enhanced concentration and productivity.

Adhere to scheduled intervals of rest: Adhering to scheduled intervals of rest promotes concentration and prevents exhaustion. Utilize your designated break times for engaging in stretching exercises, going for a leisurely stroll, or momentarily removing yourself from your workstation.

For instance, let us consider the scenario of being a student faced with an imminent and consequential examination. In order to mitigate interruptions and maintain concentration, it is advisable to establish a designated work area within your living quarters that is devoid of any disturbances. One can employ the Pomodoro Technique to allocate a period of 25 minutes for focused work, followed by a brief interval. You have the option to disable non-academic notifications on both your mobile device and computer. Utilizing noise-canceling headphones can effectively mitigate surrounding noises, enabling enhanced concentration. Furthermore, it is permissible to allocate intermittent intervals for the purpose of stretching, engaging in walking activities, or briefly stepping away from the work station.

Ultimately, the reduction of distractions and the preservation of concentration are imperative for the facilitation of efficient time allocation. By establishing a designated working area, employing the Pomodoro Technique, disabling notifications, employing noise-cancellation headphones, and incorporating periodic intervals of rest, individuals can effectively mitigate interruptions and maintain diligent concentration on their assignments, thereby enhancing productivity and accomplishing desired objectives.

## Delegation Of Duties

Distributing assignments is a highly efficient method to optimize time management and enhance overall work efficiency. By entrusting responsibilities to others, you can direct your attention towards more significant or prioritized undertakings, while others attend to less crucial matters.

In the forthcoming chapter, we shall explore the advantages of task delegation and furnish methodologies for the effective delegation of tasks.

1. The advantages of task allocation:

Assigning responsibilities yields numerous advantages, such as:

• Time efficiency: Entrusting tasks to others allows you to allocate your time towards tasks of greater significance or those with higher priority.

• Enhanced efficiency: Through the allocation of tasks, one can achieve greater productivity within a shorter timeframe, thereby augmenting overall efficiency.

• Enhanced collaboration: By assigning responsibilities, trust and effective communication can be developed, ultimately promoting improved teamwork among members of the team.

• Skill enhancement: Assigning tasks can facilitate the growth of team members' abilities, enabling them to acquire new skills or refine existing ones.

2. Effective Approaches for Delegating Tasks:

Efficient delegation necessitates concise communication, confidence in others, and a readiness to relinquish authority. Below, we present several techniques to facilitate the efficient delegation of tasks:

• Establish the parameters: Precisely establish the parameters of the task and effectively convey your expectations to the individual responsible for its completion.

• Select the appropriate individual: Take into account the individual's aptitude, expertise, and workload when assigning responsibilities. Ensure that you select an individual who possesses the necessary abilities to successfully accomplish the assigned task.

• Facilitate access to resources: Ensure the individual is equipped with the necessary resources and information to successfully accomplish the task.

• Establish a timeframe: Establish a feasible timeframe for the task and effectively convey it to the individual responsible for its completion.

• Maintain regular communication: Maintain regular communication to offer constructive feedback, address inquiries, and ascertain proper progression of the assigned task.

• Give credit: When the task is completed successfully, give credit where it is due. This fosters confidence and promotes the possibility of subsequent assignment of tasks.

Through the efficient assignment of responsibilities, one can optimize time usage, enhance overall productivity, and foster a sense of collaboration among team members.

In the forthcoming segment, we will delve into the concept of time blocking and its potential to enhance task management efficiency.

Chapter 9: Meeting Management

M

Engagements can significantly consume time if not efficiently managed. The meetings facilitate the opportunity for individuals to engage in discussions and assess whether the task is progressing satisfactorily towards the intended objective. Moreover, they encourage a thorough analysis of any potential shortcomings or deficiencies that may exist.

In this chapter, we will explore techniques for effectively overseeing meetings with the aim of optimizing time utilization and enhancing overall productivity.

The proficient handling of meetings is a necessary aptitude within the realm of time management, encompassing the strategic organization, execution, and ultimate resolution of meetings with utmost effectiveness and efficiency. Timeliness is an invaluable asset, and the prosperity of any institution hinges on its effective utilization.

Convening assemblies hold substantial significance within the operational framework of an organization, and the manner in which they are administered can exert a notable influence on productivity, decision-making processes, and the involvement of employees.

In order to effectively oversee meetings, meticulous advance planning is crucial. This encompasses the process of discerning the objective of the meeting, constructing an itinerary, extending invitations to pertinent participants, and arranging for an appropriate venue and timing.

An effectively organized meeting guarantees that all participants are fully informed of the purpose of the meeting and are able to make necessary preparations. The schedule should additionally encompass a concise delineation of subjects to be deliberated, designated time intervals for each subject, and any requisite materials or resources.

Maintaining a focused and on-track discussion is of paramount importance during the meeting. The individual responsible for leading the meeting should take measures to ensure that every participant is afforded the chance to actively contribute, and that the discourse remains in adherence to the predetermined agenda.

In addition, the leader is expected to handle any instances of disruption or disagreement that might occur, while ensuring that the meeting adheres to the designated schedule.

Furthermore, it is crucial to maximize the utilization of time throughout the course of the meeting. This entails establishing specific time constraints for each item on the agenda, succinctly outlining significant points and resolutions, and allocating subsequent responsibilities.

Through this action, the participants acquire an understanding of their obligations and can subsequently undertake appropriate measures.

Finally, it is imperative that the conclusion of the meeting be effectively overseen. This entails the concise articulation of crucial elements and conclusions reached, guaranteeing that all participants comprehend their designated responsibilities, and establishing a schedule for the subsequent gathering.

This also presents an occasion to gather valuable feedback from participants regarding the efficiency of the meeting and pinpoint areas where enhancements can be made.

Efficient management of meetings can exert a noteworthy influence on an organization's effectiveness and operational efficiency. Through the effective and efficient utilization of time, meetings can serve as a valuable instrument for both propelling progress and attaining the objectives set forth by the organization.

On the other hand, inadequately executed meetings have the potential to squander precious time, diminish participation, and impede the process of making informed decisions.

To conclude, effective meeting management is a crucial component of efficient time management, encompassing the meticulous organization, facilitation, and successful closure of meetings.

Through the implementation of optimal methodologies, such as establishing unambiguous goals, devising a well-organized agenda, proficiently allocating time, and wrapping up proceedings judiciously, companies can maximize the efficacy of their meetings and guarantee their productivity and effectiveness.

By taking such action, individuals are able to successfully accomplish their desired outcomes and objectives, whilst effectively utilizing their allocated time and resources.

In the subsequent section, we shall delve into the subject of deadline management and explore strategies for effectively adhering to project timelines.

Layman Lessons

a. Don't give up (easily)

This narrative exhibits a parallelism to the preceding one, as it showcases the fly's inclination to extensively explore the predicament in search of a resolution. On numerous occasions, we exhibit a tendency to prematurely abandon our efforts or relinquish them in close proximity to achieving desired outcomes.

It is imperative that we do not relent in our pursuit and continue to persevere in our endeavors. Alternatively, it is essential for us to acknowledge that there exist specific objectives that define our life's purpose. We must exert maximum effort in order to attain these objectives. This necessitates the qualities of tenacity and doggedness.

In order to cultivate tenacity, it is imperative to possess a commendable level of fortitude when it comes to enduring frustration. In this instance, our fly remained composed and exhibited perseverance despite being subjected to various redirections. Frequently, I engage in self-reflection when I find myself experiencing frustration over minor issues in both domestic and professional environments. Despite the child's refusal to sleep, it remains a matter of considerable frustration. At times, I experience an inclination to vigorously collide my cranium. It is impossible for anyone to possess immunity to frustration. It is imperative to combat the irregularities and inequitable treatment prevalent in the world. However, it is imperative to focus on enhancing our capacity for handling frustration. Implementing this approach will assist in mitigating frequent instances of losing our composure. Frequently, as a result of this frustration, we often opt to prematurely abandon our pursuits before attaining our desired objectives.

As an illustration, one of your crucial objectives entails avoiding any superfluous conflicts with your partner. On a particular day, your significant other requests your early presence in order to partake in an evening meal together. Nevertheless, on that very same day, your superior assigns you with the responsibility of promptly resolving an imperative document. In adherence to the commitment made to your partner, upon completing half of the assigned tasks, you kindly beseech your supervisor for a temporary release. Ultimately, you arrived at your residence with a delay of one hour beyond the anticipated time. From your perspective, it embodied the most optimal equilibrium attainable in managing your commitments to both your romantic partner and superior at work. Undoubtedly, your partner will not respond favorably and will communicate their discontent through verbal or non-verbal means. As a result, you relinquish your composure and engender confrontations. The cause of your agitation stems from the fact that, despite your diligent endeavors, the conduct exhibited by your partner fails to meet your acceptable standards. Ultimately, the degree of disagreement may differ, contingent upon the respective levels of tolerance from each party, thereby determining the outcome of your dinner. It is my contention that had you promptly offered an apology to your partner for the delay, along with an explanation of your circumstances, and demonstrated a willingness to accept any complaints or anger expressed by them, your aspiration to avoid unwarranted conflicts may have been realized.

In order to attain the utmost goals in our lives, it is imperative that we cultivate a heightened capacity for enduring frustration, much like the fly featured in this narrative.

b. Assist individuals who require assistance, in any feasible manner, no matter how slight.

In the narrative, each individual made sincere attempts to offer assistance to the fly, despite their lack of an immediate resolution. They steered the fly in the direction of the individual whom they perceived to possess greater intellect than themselves. Similar to how the tree guided the fly to seek counsel from the birds in its vicinity, the birds in turn guided it towards the expansive and sizable lake, and so forth. The crucial aspect at hand is that, should an individual in need seek our assistance in resolving their predicament and we find ourselves unable to provide a solution, there is no harm in directing them towards individuals whom we believe may offer aid. Occasionally, as exemplified in this narrative, those connections will ultimately lead the individual to the appropriate individual.

On occasion, individuals express gratitude by relaying that the legal or medical professional we recommended ultimately resolved their issue. While we may not consistently possess a recommendation nor are we compelled to provide one, should we possess a genuinely beneficial suggestion for an individual in need, there exists no justification to refrain from sharing it.

In the epic of Ramayana, Lord Rama sought the guidance and assistance of numerous individuals in his quest to confront and overcome the formidable ruler, King Ravana.

Step 3:

Setting Realistic Goals

O

After comprehending the underlying cause behind your persistent tardiness, it is imperative to establish realistic objectives that will aid in overcoming this habit. Commence on a smaller scale by discreetly disassembling considerable tasks into more manageable segments and delineating immediate objectives. This will facilitate adherence to the established course and foster the progression towards your ultimate objective.

Cultivating self-compassion is equally crucial in this regard. It is imperative to refrain from being overly critical of oneself when failing to attain these objectives. For instance, if your habitual lateness primarily originates from the tendency to procrastinate, it becomes pivotal to ascertain the underlying cause of this issue. Taking into consideration and removing possible sources of disturbance can prove to be advantageous in this particular circumstance. Identifying effective approaches that can assist in maintaining focus and dissecting tasks into more manageable components can also yield advantageous outcomes. Moreover, establishing practical deadlines for the completion of tasks may prove to be advantageous.

Establishing attainable objectives is crucial for overcoming lateness. Commence by establishing modest objectives and progressively elevating them. To guarantee the effectiveness of your goals, it is imperative to establish specific, measurable, attainable, relevant, and time-bound (SMART) objectives.

Endeavor to utilize a planner or schedule. By documenting your tasks and responsibilities throughout the day, you will enhance your ability to effectively monitor deadlines and prevent falling behind. Moreover, it is crucial to allocate additional time for task completion, thus allowing for a contingency to mitigate possible delays.

Ultimately, it is crucial to guarantee that your objectives are pragmatic and attainable. Set realistic goals and acknowledge your achievements as you progress.

Tune-Up Your Time Perception

Envision awakening in the early hours with an extensive agenda and a resolute commitment to approach each responsibility with eagerness. However, as the day progresses, you encounter difficulties maintaining concentration and face challenges in accurately gauging the duration of each task. Prior to one's awareness, the afternoon has already advanced, leaving a substantial portion of one's assignments unfinished. This phenomenon of time blindness experienced by individuals with ADHD presents the truth of their situation, and I can personally empathize with the inherent challenges.

Articulating the exasperation arising from the inability to effectively maintain a precise record of time can pose a challenge when conveying this sentiment to others. This is why it is crucial to possess a support network that comprehends the situation and can provide efficacious methodologies to effectively handle time. It does not pertain to indolence or insufficiency of creativity; rather, it involves grappling with executive functioning capabilities and a distinct perception of time.

After engaging in a process of experimentation and learning, I have identified and implemented effective strategies to successfully mitigate the effects of time blindness. One approach that I especially endorse is the method of decomposing larger tasks into more manageable and achievable increments. This affords me the capability to sustain focus and drive, as I am able to witness incremental advancements. Furthermore, the incorporation of visual aids, such as the utilization of timers or the implementation of color-coded calendars, has proven to be effective in facilitating my time management skills. With the aid of a physical manifestation of the passage of time, I am able to more accurately gauge the duration of a task and subsequently organize my schedule in a more effective manner.

It is imperative to bear in mind that time blindness is a manifestation of ADHD, rather than an indication of personal inadequacy. With adequate assistance, comprehensive approaches, pharmaceutical interventions, and therapeutic modalities, individuals with ADHD can transcend this condition.

Exercise: Tick Tock Tracking

Presented below is a pragmatic task intricately crafted to facilitate the enhancement of time estimation and management abilities among individuals diagnosed with ADHD:

1. Please provide accurate time estimations while considering the possibility of both underestimating or overestimating the duration of tasks.

2. Utilize a timer or chronometer to monitor and record the duration required for the accomplishment of each individual task.

3. Take into consideration any disparities between the time you initially

projected and the time you ultimately spent, and contemplate the possible reasons for such variations.

4. Please indicate a minimum of one approach that you could employ to enhance your ability to effectively estimate and regulate your time in subsequent endeavors.

5. Implement this approach in your subsequent assignments and take note of any enhancements in time management and productivity.

Allow me to present an illustrative example to enhance comprehension:

Today's agenda consists of tidying the bedroom and completing a professional work report.

Please document every task and provide an estimation of the time required for completion.

● Engaging in the task of tidying up your bedroom: a dedicated time period of 30 minutes

● Completion of a work report: 60 minutes

Utilize a chronometer or timepiece to monitor the duration required for the completion of each task.

● Arranging the tidiness of your bedroom: Estimated time required - 45 minutes

● Completion of a work report: 75 minutes

Please assess any disparities between your projected time and the actual time elapsed, and contemplate upon them.

● The task of tidying your bedroom exceeded your initial time estimation, as you became inadvertently absorbed in the process of arranging your closet.

● The completion of the work report exceeded the estimated time frame due to the necessity of conducting supplementary research.

Please determine a minimum of one approach that you can apply to enhance your ability to accurately assess and effectively handle your time in subsequent instances.

● Decompose the cleaning tasks into smaller sequential stages and allocate distinct timeframes for each stage.

● It would be advisable to allocate supplementary time for conducting research pertaining to work-related responsibilities in order to account for unforeseen hindrances.

Implement this approach in your subsequent array of assignments and meticulously monitor any advancements in time management and productivity.

● As an illustration, when engaging in the task of kitchen cleaning, it is advisable to deconstruct the process into sequential actions (such as washing dishes, wiping counters, and sweeping) while allocating precise durations for each.

Please be advised that this activity is intended to facilitate your understanding of your perception of time and your personal habits, while also allowing you to determine the most effective strategies for yourself. There is no need for concern if you encounter some experimental attempts before identifying an effective approach; what truly matters is your proactive initiative in striving for improved time management.

Utilize a productivity application or utility to monitor and enhance progress while maintaining motivation

In the midst of traversing the complexities of the rapidly evolving digital landscape, the task of upholding productivity and efficiently managing one's time often appears to be a daunting challenge. Amidst an array of approaches aimed at optimizing productivity, the utilization of a productivity application or tool has emerged as a widely embraced and efficacious methodology. Through the strategic utilization of technological advancements, we have the opportunity to optimize our workflow, uphold a sense of orderliness, and cultivate a high level of drive, consequently bolstering our overall efficiency and efficacy.

A productivity application is a software program or platform specifically developed to enhance the efficiency and effectiveness with which individuals or groups complete their tasks. These applications can encompass a broad spectrum of functionalities, ranging from the management of tasks and planning of projects to the monitoring of time and facilitating communication. By offering a structured and centralized platform for task management, these applications have the potential to markedly alleviate the cognitive burden associated with engaging in multiple tasks and switching between them. Consequently, this enables individuals to conserve mental energy and devote it to more concentrated and productive endeavors.

In the realm of task management, productivity applications have the potential to dramatically transform efficiency and performance. These applications can provide a distinct visual portrayal of your workload, as they enable you to generate, classify, arrange, and monitor tasks. This can aid in maintaining organization, efficiently managing time, and mitigating the risk of tasks being overlooked. Furthermore, through offering a concise outline of your duties and their respective advancements, these applications have the capability to sustain motivation by allowing you to distinctly discern the outcomes of your exertions.

Productivity applications may also encompass functionalities related to time monitoring. These attributes have the ability to offer valuable understanding regarding the allocation of your time, thereby aiding in the identification of recurring tendencies, hindrances, and advantageous prospects for enhancement. As an example, it may come to your attention that specific assignments are exceeding the estimated timeframe, or that an excessive amount of time is being allocated to tasks that hold lesser significance. By offering this valuable perspective, the implementation of time tracking can facilitate better and more proficient decision-making pertaining to the prioritization of tasks and the management of time.

Furthermore, aside from task management and time tracking, numerous productivity applications also provide functionalities for communication and collaboration. This can offer considerable advantages for teams, as it facilitates efficient communication, consolidation of information, and coordinated management of tasks. By facilitating effective communication and promoting collaboration, these applications have the potential to enhance team efficiency and strengthen unity within the group.

While productivity applications can provide a plethora of advantages, it is imperative to select an application that corresponds with your individual requirements, professional methodology, and personal inclinations. The most suitable productivity application for you will be contingent upon a multitude of factors, encompassing the nature of your profession, the scope of your workforce, your favored approach to work, and your individual inclinations. When choosing an application, it is advisable to take into account its functionalities, user interface, user-friendliness, compatibility with other software, and the level of customer assistance provided.

Additionally, although productivity applications have the potential to greatly improve productivity, they are not a panacea. A dedication to productivity and cultivation of exemplary work habits are essential for utilizing these tools efficiently. It is imperative to integrate the utilization of productivity applications with additional productivity methodologies, including time management methodologies, periodic intervals of rest, and the cultivation of a harmonious work-life equilibrium.

In summary, productivity applications can prove to be a potent asset within your repertoire for enhancing productivity. Through the provision of a structured and consolidated framework for task management, time tracking, and communication facilitation, these tools possess the capacity to heighten proficiency, sustain drive, and ultimately, uplift productivity. Nevertheless, it is crucial to bear in mind that these tools simply serve as instruments. The efficacy of these tools is contingent upon their utilization and should be synergistically paired with exemplary work practices and proficient productivity techniques to yield optimal advantages.

## Conquering Your Tendency To Put Things Off

Procrastination is a problem that many people experience, and it may have a significant negative effect on an individual's productivity as well as their level of success. Delaying duties and avoiding obligations is a tendency that can lead to missed deadlines, frustration, and a sensation of being overburdened. This habit is known as procrastination. Procrastination, on the other hand, is something that can be conquered with the use of the appropriate tactics and mentality.

Having an understanding of the fundamental reasons behind procrastination: To be successful in overcoming procrastination, one must first comprehend the underlying reasons behind their behavior. It's possible that this is due to a fear of failing, perfectionism, a lack of drive, or simply the fact that they are too busy with other activities. Individuals are able to find ways to address their behavior and find solutions to overcome it if they first understand the underlying cause of the problem.

Taking chores one at a time The sensation that you are unable to complete a major activity in its whole is a common contributor to procrastination. Individuals can prevent themselves from feeling overwhelmed and achieve progress in a manner that is more bearable if the activities at hand are broken down into smaller, more manageable parts.

Keeping a task list can assist individuals in prioritizing their work and monitoring their level of completion, which can be accomplished through the use of a task list. This can enhance motivation and aid in overcoming procrastination because it provides a goal that is obvious and can be accomplished.

Setting a deadline is an effective way to boost motivation and maintain concentration on a certain endeavor (such as completing an assignment). Individuals are provided with a distinct goal to work towards and are able to eliminate the temptation to engage in procrastination when a deadline is established.

Altering our surroundings can have a significant impact, both positively and negatively, on our behavior and our levels of motivation. Individuals are able to improve their motivation and level of concentration on their duties by altering their environments and designing workspaces that are more conducive to productivity.

Changing an individual's thinking and attitude toward activities can have a significant impact on their motivation and capacity to overcome procrastination. Individuals can enhance their motivation and conquer procrastination by adopting a growth mindset and perceiving problems as chances for growth.

Individuals can overcome procrastination and boost their productivity and success by first gaining a knowledge of the fundamental reason of their procrastination, then breaking down work, making use of a task list, setting deadlines, altering their environment, and adopting a growth mindset. These steps are in addition to changing the environment. Individuals are able to overcome procrastination and achieve their goals in a manner that is more effective and efficient if they put these tactics into practice and put them into action.

Conclusively, overcoming procrastination is an essential component of effective time management that can have a significant influence on one's productivity as well as their level of success. Individuals are able to overcome procrastination and enhance their motivation and focus on their goals if they first identify the underlying reason of the problem, then break down the activities at hand, create a list of the things they need to complete, establish deadlines, and adopt a growth mindset.

Individuals can educate their thoughts to adopt a more productive and focused approach to the tasks they need to do by constantly practicing these tactics. Although overcoming the habit of procrastination might be challenging, it is possible to do so. Individuals are able to overcome procrastination and more easily and effectively attain their goals if they are patient and persistent throughout the process.

www.ingramcontent.com/pod-product-compliance
Lightning Source LLC
Chambersburg PA
CBHW052139110526
44591CB00012B/1786